Descriptive Words For Writers: Places

PIPER BRADLEY

ISBN: 1530633559
ISBN-13: 978-1530633555

CONTENTS

INTRODUCTION

If you are like me, you've been reading craft books that tell you to 'write descriptive' sentences. You've learned that you need to use action verbs that evoke a specific sense of time and place. But *how* do you do that?

Start with this book (and hopefully this series).

In this book, you will find a list of places like Mountains and Forests, as well as descriptive words to evoke the senses (sight, sound, smell, touch and taste). In many places, taste will be at a minimum, because let's face it, when it comes to taste, usually it means you're sitting down to eat or drink.

Whenever it's possible, I've included taste, but the majority of 'taste' words will be in the next book, *Descriptive Words for Writers: People.*

How to use this book:

Pick on a Place that you wish to describe.

Read through the list of words and envision your scene.

To determine the kinds of activities you can do in that Place, select the next section, 'Actions'.

Continue visualizing as you read through the next sections 'Touch', 'Scents', 'Sounds' and where applicable, 'Taste'.

This book is aimed to get you thinking about and writing your scene using descriptive words. I would always recommend doing some basic research on a specific place, as descriptions can vary based on location.

If you have any comments, questions, or critiques, feel free to email me at piperbradley35@gmail.com..

1 MOUNTAINS (SIGHT)

What kinds of things would you SEE in or on a mountain? How would you describe a mountain? Pick some of the words below:

Alp
Alpine
Altitude
Ascent

***

Bank
Barren
Bedrock
Behemoth
Bluff
Boulder
Bulk
Bundle
Butte

***

Cave
Cliff
Colossus
Crag
Craggy
Crevasse
Crusty

Culvert

***

Deposit
Depression
Dip
Dirty
Dome
Dusty

***

Earth
Earthy
Elevation
Escarpment

***

Falling rocks

***

Glob
Goliath
Graded
Gradually

***

Haul
Heap
Heave
Hill
Hill
Hillock
Hump

***

Lava
Leviathan
Load

***

Magma
Mammoth
Mass
Mesa
Mine
Mineral

Mound
Mount

***

Palisade
Peak
Pike
Pitch (steep section)
Platform
Precipice
Pyramid

***

Quarry

***

Range
Ridge
Rise
Rock
Rock slides
Roof

***

Sheer
Shock
Sierra
Slab
Slope
Snow capped
Stack
Steep

***

Titan
Ton
Top
Trees
Tunnel

***

Uplift

***

Valley
Volcano

Volume

***

Whole

2 MOUNTAINS (ACTIONS)

This list contains action words that your Character(s) can do in or on a Mountain. Do not forget about the creatures (and plants) that live in or on a Mountain. They are just as active as your Character(s), so be sure to describe their actions as well.

Advance
Ascend

***

Belay/ Belaying (climbing technique)
Break up
Burrow

***

Careen
Clamber
Clean (up, off)
Climb
Collide
Continue
Crawl
Cut

***

Descend
Dig
Discover
Drive

Drop

***

Empty
Enter
Excavate
Exhume
Explore

***

Fall
Falter
Find
Flounder

***

Go down
Go into
Gouge

***

Hesitate
Hollow (out)
Hunt

***

Ignore
Inspect
Investigate

***

Jump

***

Limp
Look into
Lower
Lumber
Lurch

***

Mine
Misjudge

***

Neglect

***

Overlook

***

Peer into
Penetrate
Pierce
Pitch
Probe
Push

***

Reel
Retreat
Roam
Root (out)
Run

***

Scale
Scoop (out)
Scout
Scrape
Scrutinize
Search
Seek
Shift
Shove
Shovel
Sift
Slide
Slip
Slump
Soak (hot springs)
Splash
Stooping
Stumble
Sweat
Swim (hot springs)
Swing

***

Test
Till
Tilt

Topple
Traverse
Trip (as in fall)
Try
Tunnel
Turn over

***

Uncover
Unearth

***

Walk
Waver

3 MOUNTAINS (TOUCH)

In the pitch black darkness, what does a
Mountain/Cave/Tunnel FEEL like?

Abrasive
Blunt
Broken
Bumpy

***

Choppy
Coarse
Cold
Complete
Craggy
Crude
Crusty

***

Dry

***

Easy
Even
Flat
Fuzzy

***

Gentle

***

Hairy
Harsh

***

Incline
Incomplete

***

Irregular

***

Jagged

***

Knobby
Knotty

***

Long

***

Polished

***

Raised
Refined
Ridged
Rocky
Rough
Ruffled
Rugged

***

Scraggy
Scratchy
Sharp
Short
Slippery
Smooth
Soft
Spiky / Spikes
Steep
Stony

***

Tangled
Tough

***

Unequal
Uneven
Unfinished

***

Wet
Wrinkled

NOTE: for a complete list of Textures, check out the **TEXTURES Master List** on page 257.

4 MOUNTAINS (SOUNDS)

What kinds of SOUNDS would you hear in a cave just beyond the tunnel you are in?

Dripping (water / blood -Horror)

***

Echo

***

Hear yourself breathing

***

Quiet

***

Scuffling
Scurrying
Shuffling
Splash

***

Waterfall (rushing)
Weeping
Wind whistling

NOTE: Check out the Master List of Animal Sounds on page 227.

PIPER BRADLEY

5 MOUNTAINS (SMELL)

If your Mountain has caves, you can choose any of the scents below. If it is a Mountain without caves, the scents will depend on if the Mountain is covered in trees or craggy rocks. It will depend on the wildlife that inhabit your particular mountain. Most likely, the air will be fresh and clean. Unless you are climbing an active volcano. So think about your specific Mountain and then decide if any of the following words apply to you:

Animal musk

***

Bat droppings

***

Clean (if no bats are present)
Crisp

***

Damp

***

Earthy

***

Fetid
Fresh

***

Musty

***

Refreshing

***

Sour
Stagnant (air)
Stale (air)
Sulfur (Thermal or hot springs)

***

Wet

Note: Be sure to check the **Scents Master List** on page 249.

6 MOUNTAINS (TASTE)

When it comes to taste, usually it means you're sitting down to eat or drink. What you are eating and drinking largely depends on the specific location, time period and type of animal available. This section is thin, however, a complete list of TASTE descriptors (the **Master List of Taste)** is located toward the end of this book.

You decide where you want a source of water (if you want one) and how you want your readers to respond to the setting you chose.

A stream (any flowing water) could be:
Cool
Crisp
Fresh
Refreshing

A body of water that was still could be:
Putrid
Rancid
Stagnant
Stale
Tainted

(Imagine a stagnant body of water full of bat droppings.)

NOTE: For a complete list of TASTE descriptors, check out the **Master List of Taste** on page 213.

7 CAVES

What kinds of things would you find in a Cave? The following words are Cave specific, but there is some overlap with Tunnels and Mountains.

Bat droppings
Bats
Burrow

***

Catacomb
Cavern
Cavity
Cell
Chilly
Compartment
Concave
Covered with feces
Crystal clear water

***

Damp
Dank
Darkness
Den

***

Falling rocks
Flooding

Flowstone
Fountain

           ***

Grave
Grotto

           ***

Hovel
Humid
Hypothermia

           ***

Jet

           ***

Lair
Littered with bones

           ***

Mausoleum
Mud
Muggy

           ***

Pitch (steep section)
Pitch Black
Pothole

           ***

Rainwater (flooding)
Retreat
Room

           ***

Sand
Sepulcher
Shelter
Silt
Spa
Spout
Squeeze(s)
Stagnant water /pool
Stalactite (forms on the ceiling of caves)
Stalagmite (forms on the floor of caves by dripping water)
Steamy
Stream

Subterranean

***

Thermal (hot) spring
Tomb
Tunnel

***

Vault

***

Water hazard(s)
Well
Wet

8 ICE CAVES

Ice caves can be permanently frozen year round or temporarily frozen during the winter season, if conditions are right. Do your research! Here are some words to get you visualizing:

Accumulated snow (forms ice that is course, crystalline, looks like glacier ice)

***

Below freezing
Blue green color of Ice
Brinicles (ice stalactites that form under sea ice)

***

Cavity
Chamber(s)
Cliffs (depends on where the cave is formed)
Cold traps
Crystals

***

Delicate Arches
Dense air

***

Falling Ice formations (danger)
Frost crystals
Frost Feathers
Frozen waterfalls

***

Getting lost in the tunnels / labyrinth / maze (Danger)
Glacier cave
Glare Ice

***

Honeycombed passages / tunnels

***

Ice
Ice Avalanche
Ice Cleats
Ice columns (forms when icicles and stalagmites combine)
Ice draperies
Ice formations (icicles, stalagmites, ice columns, frozen
waterfall)
Ice plates
Icicles / Ice Stalactites
Intrusions

***

Labyrinth
Lava tube
Limestone Cave

***

Maze

***

Needle ice

***

Permafrost
Ponded water (forms clear ice mass when frozen)

***

Scalloped walls (of Ice)
Ski pole / Walking stick
Snow cracks
Snow mounds
Stalagmites

***

Translucent walls (of ice)
Tunnels

***

Uneven terrain

***

Vaulted Chambers

***

Wind Chill

TOUCH

What does an Ice Cave feel like? Hopefully you are wearing gloves, but you could still feel:

Bumpy

Cold

Freezing

Slippery
Smooth

SOUNDS

Through your earmuffs, if you hear a loud crack, get out of there fast!

Loud Crack

ACTION in an Ice Cave

This list contains things that you can do in an ice cave as well as what the ice can do to you. Beware!

Collapse (rock, ice falling, a person fainting)
Cover (eyes, head etc)
Crouch

Falling (debris)

Glisten (Ice)

Rain down (debris)

Scattering (run away from dangerous icicles falling)
Slip
Stand

9 TUNNELS

What are some ways to describe Tunnels? The following words are Tunnel specific, but there is some overlap with Caves and Mountains.

Airflow
Aqueduct
Arroyo
Artery
Avenue

***

Blast
Burrow

***

Canal
Canyon
Chamber
Channel
Conduit
Corridors
Course
Crawlspace
Crawlway
Crevice
Crosscut
Current

***

Ditch
Draft
Drift
Drop-off
Duct

***

Fluting
Fork (out)
Furrow

***

Gouge (out)
Groove
Gully
Gust
Gutter

***

Hole
Hole in the Wall
Honeycomb

***

Labyrinth
Ledges

***

Main
Man-made
Maze
Medium
Mine

***

Natural

***

Pass
Passage
Path
Pathway
Pierce
Pipe
Pit

Puncture

***

Route
Runway

***

Sand
Sewer
Shaft
Silt
Sink
Slit
Strait
Subway

***

Tideway
Tight Passages
Trail
Trough
Tube

***

Underpass

***

Vein
Ventilation

***

Waft
Way
Whiff

10 VOLCANOES

Ashes
                                * * *

Basalt
Bedrock
Boulder
                                * * *

Cinders
Cobblestone
Crag
Crevasse
Crust
                                * * *

Depression
Dross
                                * * *

Earth
Elevation
                                * * *

Gravel
                                * * *

Hot
                                * * *

Lava
Lodge
                                * * *

Magma
Mass
Mesa
Metal
Mineral

     ***

Obsidian
Ore

     ***

Pebble
Pyramid

     ***

Quarry

     ***

Reef
Refuse
Residue
Rubble

     ***

Shelf
Sierra
Slab
Slag

11 DESERT (SIGHT)

Below are a list of things that you would see in a generic Desert. Do your research to determine the specific plants and animal life you would find in your specific Desert. Does your world include a "normal" desert, like the Sahara, or a Polar desert like Antarctica?

Abraded (rocks)
Addax (Antelope)
Agave
Alluvial fan
Alluvium
Anticline
Ants
Arid
Arroyo (Dry stream channel / desert gully)
***
Bajada
Baked soil
Barchan dunes (crescent shaped)
Barren
Bedrock
Beetles
Blaze
Bleak
Blooms

Blowout
Bone-dry
Brittlebush

***

Camels
Campfire
Canyons
Caravans
Charring
Clay
Cliff
Coarse silt
Couch's Spadefoot Toad
Coyote

***

Dangerous
Den
Desert pavement
Desert Rain Frog
Desert rat
Desert Shrimp
Desert varnish
Deserted
Desolate
Detritus
Dikdik
Dome dunes
Dormant animals
Dormant seeds
Downpours (occasional)
Drought
Dry
Dunes
Dung
Dust devil
Dust storm
Dusty

***

Embers

Empty
Erosion (wind, water)
Expansive
Exposed bedrock

***

Fairy Shrimp
False Mesquite
Fierce
Fire
Fissures
Flame
Flare
Flash flood
Flat, stone covered plains
Fleshy tubers
Flies
Forsaken
Fragments (of rock)

***

Glittering (sand)
Glow
Grant's Gazelle

***

Hawks
Heat
Hogback
Hoodoo
Hostile
Hot

***

Inferno
Infertile

***

Jackal
Jerboas

***

Kangaroo rat
Kit Fox

***

Lifeless
Locusts
Loess
Lonely

***

Match
Maze
Medium grain sand
Mesa
Millipedes
Monocline
Mosaic (consisting of smooth stones)
Mountains
Mysterious

***

Never-ending
Nocturnal animals
Nomads (Bushmen in the Kalahari, Aborigines in
Austrailia, Indian tribes in North America - research history)

***

Oasis
Oryx

***

Parched
Pediment
Pillars
Pinnacles
Plants (wiry, small, no leaves, cacti)
Playa
Polar desert
Prickly Pear

***

Quiet

***

Ravines
Rippling
Rocks
Rubble

***

Saharan Silver ant
Sand
Sand dunes
Sand storm
Sandgrouse
Scorpions
Seif dunes (linear)
Shade
Shadow
Shallow roots
Short woody trees
Shrubs
Slabs
Slaves (historically slaves were transported via Sahara desert)
Smoke
Snake
Solar energy panels (Mojave desert)
Solitary
Sparks
Spiders
Spines (on cacti)
Star dunes
Sterile
Succulent leaves
Sunny
Syncline

***

Taproots (if you dig)
Temporary lake(s)
Tents (made of animal skin)
Termites
Tinder
Tough Plants
Trade routes
Traders
Transverse dunes
Tunnels (of animals)
Turpentine bush

***

Underground river or lake
Underground sources of water (springs)
Uninhabited
Unspoiled
Untamed

***

Very fine sand
Virgin (unexplored territory)

***

Waste (land)
Water Holding Frog
Water resistant plants
Wild
Wind
Windblown
Wiry Plants

***

Yucca

POLAR DESERT

Arid

Blizzards

Drifts

Ice

Salty earth
Snow
Snow dunes
Strong winds

12 DESERT (ACTIONS)

This list contains action words that your Character(s) can do in a Desert. Do not forget about the creatures (and plants) that live in a Desert. They are just as active as your Character(s), so be sure to describe their actions as well.

Abrade
Argue

***

Bargain
Barter
Build a fire
Burning
Burrow
Buy

***

Deal
Dehydrate
Die
Dig
Distribute
Drink

***

Exchange

***

Finding (water)
Flood
Forage
Freeze

***

Graze

***

Harden
Herding (sheep, goats, cattle, camels, yaks, llamas, reindeer)
Hide
Hike
Hunger

***

Ice (cover with ice)

***

Lie dormant

***

Mining

***

Numb

***

Persuade

***

Rest
Rock climbing

***

Scorching
Searching (for water)
Sell
Set up tents
Shatter (rocks)
Shiver
Smuggle
Solidify
Study
Sunburn
Survive

***

Think
Thirsty
Tracking (animals)
Trade
Trafficking

13 DESERT (TOUCH)

Think about all the things you can touch in the Desert of your imagination. Describe them using the words below:

Abrasive

***

Broken (rocks)
Bumpy

***

Cool
Crude

***

Dry

***

Feathery
Fine (sand)
Formless
Freezing
Furry
Fuzzy

***

Grainy
Gravelly
Gritty

***

Hard
Harsh

***

Icy

***

Jagged

***

Polished

***

Ridged
Rocky
Rough
Rugged

***

Scorching
Sharp
Short
Smooth
Spiky
Stiff

***

Tough

***

Uneven

***

Wet (rarely)
Withered
Wool / Woolly
Wrinkled

NOTE: for a complete list of Textures, check out the **TEXTURES Master List** on page 257.

14 DESERT (SOUNDS)

The sounds you hear in your desert depends on where it's located, time of year and the situation surrounding your character. A character who has been captured and is now part of a human trafficking ring in the distant past will hear different sounds than that of a Nomad or a modern visitor.

Baa
Bark
Bay (animal sounds)
Bleating
Braying (various animals)

***

Chattering
Chirp
Clicking (beetles)
Cluck
Crackling (fire)
Croak (if toad is not dormant)

***

Growl

***

Hiss (snake)
Hoot
Howl (coyote, wind)

***

Popping (fire)

***

Rushing sound of Wind

***

Snort (camels)
Squawk

***

Warbling
Whistling (Wind)
Wind

***

Yip
Yowl

NOTE: Check out the Master List of Animal Sounds on page 227.

15 DESERT (SMELL)

The scents your character encounter depends on where it's located, time of year and the situation surrounding your character. A character who has been captured and is now part of a human trafficking ring in the distant past will smell different scents than that of a Nomad or a modern visitor. Keep that in mind as you peruse the list below.

Animal musk (camels, birds, sheep etc.)

***

Burnt wood

***

Delicate
Delightful
Distinct

***

Faint
Foul
Fragrant (when flowers are blooming)

***

Gamy
Grody
Gross

***

Infected (think of victims of human trafficking)
Intense

***

Lasting
Light

***

Mellow
Mild
Musk

***

Natural

***

Overpowering
Overwhelming

***

Pleasant

***

Reek
Revolting
Ripe (as in stinky)
Roasted

***

Smoke
Subtle
Sweaty
Sweet

***

Unfamiliar

Note: Be sure to check the **Scents Master List** on page
249.

16 DESERT (TASTE)

When it comes to taste, usually it means you're sitting down to eat or drink. What you are eating and drinking largely depends on the specific location, time period and type of animal available. This section is thin, however, a complete list of TASTE descriptors (the **Master List of Taste)** is located toward the end of this book.

Blood

Meat
Milk

Parched

Refreshing

Thirsty

NOTE: For a complete list of TASTE descriptors, check out the **Master List of Taste** on page 213.

17 FOREST (SIGHT)

Below are a list of things that you would see in a generic Forest. Do your research to determine the specific plants and animal life you would find in your specific Forest.

Animal bones
Animal prints
Animals (depends on where the forest is located- think of specific birds, mammals, reptiles, insects)

***

Backwoods
Bark
Berries
Berries
Birds (Owls, Robins, Loons etc.)
Blade
Blossoms
Bramble
Branches
Briar
Brood
Bruised
Brush
Buds
Bugs

Burrow
Bush

***

Campfire
Camping
Canopy (harshest layer, home to birds, tree frogs, snakes, lizards, hard-bodied insects)
Carpets
Cascades
Case (seed)
Chaparral
Char
Clumps
Coat (seed)
Color (depends on the type of tree/flower, season. Do your research)
Common
Covert
Creeper
Crowded
Curled

***

Deer
Den
Dew
Die
Disease
Drab
Draught
Drooping
Dying

***

Eggs
Embers
Erosion

***

Fade
Fir
Flame
Flock
Flowers (be specific as to the type)
Fog
Footpath
Footprints
Forest Floor Layer (leaf litter, soil, insects, worms, slugs, spiders, microbes)
Fork in the road/path
Fountains
Frond
Frost

***

Ghosts
Grass
Green
Grove
Growth

***

Hedge
Herbaceous Layer (mosses, flowers)
Herbs
Herd (of mammals like Deer)
Hole
Husk

***

Insects (Mosquitoes, Bees, Moths, Butterflies)
Invasive
Ivy

***

Jungle

***

Labyrinth
Lair
Lake

Leaves
Lifeless
Lime
Log

***

Majestic
Mammals (Deer, Bears, Wolves etc.)
Mats
Maze
Mediocre
Mist
Moles
Moss
Mottled
Mounds
Mythical or Monstrous creatures

***

Natives (Is there a group of people that live in the forest?)
Needle
Nest

***

Old
Olive
Ordinary
Outback
Overgrown

***

Pack (of wolves)
Parasite
Park
Partially decomposing animals
Path
pests
Petal
Pine
Plain

Plant
Poison Ivy
Poison Oak
Poison Sumac
Poisonous
Pond
Poor drainage
Primeval
Problem areas
Pulp

***

Reptiles (snakes, lizards, alligators)
River
Roasting Marshmallows
Rodents
Roots
Rosette (leaf arrangement)
Route
Rows

***

Sag
Sage
Sap
Sapling
School
Scorched
Scrub
Seedling
Seeds
Shadows
Shape of Leaves, petals (round, long, heart shaped,
rounded, ear shaped, wedge shaped, slanting, kidney shaped, thin)
Shelter
Shoot(s)
Shortcut
Shrub Layer (Insects, spiders, birds, snakes, lizards live
here)
Shrubbery

Sleeping bags
Sliver
Smoke
Sparks
Speckled
Splinter
Spotted
Stalk
Stinging Nettle
Stream
Stump
Sun
Swarm

***

Tangle
Tent
Thick / Dense / Impenetrable
Thicket
Thorns
Tiers
Timber
Timberline
Topiary
Towering
Trail(s)
Tree (be specific as to the type)
Trunk
Twigs
Twisted

***

Undergrowth
Understory (layer under the Canopy, variety of animals live
here: birds, butterflies/caterpillars, frogs, mammals)
Unstable

***

Variegated
Veined
Vine

***

Weak
Wilderness
Willow
Wilt
Wind
Wither
Withered
Wood
Woodland
Woods
Wrinkly

18 FOREST (ACTIONS)

This list contains action words that your Character(s) can do in the forest. Do not forget about the creatures (and plants) that live in the forest. They are just as active as your Character(s), so be sure to describe their actions as well.

Analyze
Arched

***

Backpacking
Bet
Blocked
Burn
Burrow
Burst
Bury
Bushwhacking (may carry a negative connotation)

***

Catch
Chase
Choked
Chop (down)
Climb
Cloaked
Cover up
Covered

Crept
Cross
Cross over
Crouch
Cut

***

Danced
Destroy
Ditch (as in drop or get rid of)
Droop

***

Erupted
Examine
Explore
Exposed to sunlight

***

Find
Fishing
Floated
Fluttered
Follow
Forage

***

Get
Grab
Grasped

***

Hide
Hike
Hop
Hopped
Horseback Riding
Hung
Hunt
Hurt

***

Ignore
Inspect
Investigate
Itch

***

Keep Watch
Kill
Knotted

***

Lit
Lurk

***

Maim
March

***

Nab
Nail
Note
Notice

***

Obscure
Observe

***

Pass over
Pass through
Patrol
Perch
Pick (fruit)
Plan
Plant
Pluck (berries, fruits)
Probe
Protect
Pursue

***

Ramble
Relax
Reveal
Roost
Rose
Run

***

Sag
Scamper
Scramble
Scratch
Scratched
Search
Secure
Seduce
Seek
Seize
Separate
Shake
Shook
Shout
Shrouded
Slash
Slink
Slog
Sneak
Spot
Spread
Spy
Stash
Stood
Store
Strangled
Stretched
Stroll
Study
Survey
Swayed

Swing

***

Take
Tangled
Test
Threaten
Tossed
Tour
Tramping
Trapped
Trekking
Trespass
Trick
Twisted

***

Uncover
Unearth

***

Walk
Wander
Watch
Whisper
Wilt
Wither
Wriggled
Writhed

19 FOREST (TOUCH)

Think about all the things you can touch in the forest of your imagination. Leaves, bark, flowers, rocks. Describe them using the words below:

Barbed
Blunt
Bristly

***

Dry

***

Felt (type of fabric)
Finely toothed
Fringed with hairs

***

Grooves

***

Hairy
Harsh

***

Jagged

***

Leathery

***

Pointed
Prickly

***

Rough
Rounded

***

Saw toothed
Shallow toothed
Sharp
Sharp, rigid tip
Silky
Smooth
Spiky
Stiff, sharp points
Succulent

***

Thorny
Toothed
Tough

***

Veined
Velvety

***

Wavy toothed
Waxy
Woolly

NOTE: for a complete list of Textures, check out the **TEXTURES Master List** on page 257.

To describe the shapes of leaves or petals, refer to **Leaves and Petals Description** on page 235.

20 FOREST (SOUNDS)

Barking
Bay (dogs or wolves)
Bellow (Moose, deer)
Bleat (calves)
Bray
Bubbling (brook)
Bugle (Elk)
Buzzing

***

Cawing (crows)
Chatter (birds)
Chirp (Cicadas)
Chirping
Clamor
Clattering bills (birds)
Crackling (from campfire)
Croaking
Crunching (leaves)
Cry

***

Footsteps

***

Growl

***

Hiss (snake)
Honk
Hoot
Howl
Humming

***

Neigh (horse)

***

Pop / popping (from campfire)

***

Quacking

***

Rain falling
Roar
Rustling

***

Scampering
Scrambling
Scratching
Scream (Vulture)
Screech
Shriek
Shuffling
Snapping (twigs)
Snort (deer)
Squeak
Swish (leaves)

***

Toot
Trill (Raccoons)
Trumpet
Tweeting

***

Wail

Woodpecker drumming, hammering, pounding

***

Yelp

NOTE: Check out the **Master List of Animal Sounds** on page 227.

21 FOREST (SMELL)

Once again, I must caution you to think about what kind of forest you are describing. A Rain Forest will smell differently from a forest of Pine trees. Here are a few words to get you thinking about scents:

Cedar
Clean / Fresh (after rain)
Cypress

***

Decay
Decomposition (animal)
Decomposition (leaves)
Douglas Fir (lemony, pineapple, floral scent)

***

Floral scents (depends on the type of forest)

***

Gamy

***

Moldy
Musk (animal)

***

Pine

***

Rot (wood, animals)

***

Smoke (campfire)

***

Woody, camphor

Note: Be sure to check the **Scents Master List** on page 249.

22 FOREST (TASTE)

When it comes to taste, usually it means you're sitting down to eat or drink. What you are eating and drinking largely depends on the specific location, time period and type of animal available. A complete list of TASTE descriptors (the **Master List of Taste)** is located on page 213.

Acidic

***

Bitter
Burnt (cooked food)

***

Cherry flavored
Clean
Comforting (pair this with comfort foods)
Coppery
Cough Syrup

***

Delicate
Distinctive
Dry (overcooked food)

***

Earthy
Exotic

***

Familiar
Flavorful
Foul
Fruity

***

Gamy
Gross

***

Lemon / Lemony
Lingering (aftertaste)

***

Mild
Minty
Moist (perfectly cooked food)

***

Overpowering
Overripe

***

Peculiar
Pure

***

Refreshing
Rich
Ripe
Rotten

***

Salty
Satisfying
Savory
Smoky
Sour
Spicy
Spoiled
Subtle
Sweet (berries)

***

Tangy

23 RAINFOREST

Abundance
Acid rain
Amazon River

***

Bacteria
Bats (Emergent Layer)
Biodiversity
Birds
Boa constrictors (Understory layer)
Bugs
Butterflies (Emergent Layer)
Buzz

***

Canopy
Catastrophe
Chameleons
Colorful (feathers, animals)
Criminals
Crowded (trees/plants grow close together)

***

Damage
Debris
Decay
Decaying (plant and animal)
Decline

Deforestation
Dense undergrowth
Disease

**

Eagles (Emergent layer)
Emergent Layer (very tall trees)
Endangered Animals

**

Farmers
Feathers
Food chain (think about what you would see)
Forest floor
Fungi

**

Habitat
Humid
Hunters

Jaguars (Understory layer)
Jungle

**

Leopards (understory layer)
Lizards
Loggers
Low light (forest floor)

**

Medicines
Monkeys (some live in the Emergent Layer)
Monsoon
Natives / tribes
Nests

**

Orchids

Parasite
Predators
Primeval
Pristine

***

Rain
Rainwater
Ranchers
Rapid decay
Riverbanks
Rivers
Roads

***

Shrub layer
Shrubs
Small trees
Snakes

***

Threatened Animals
Tree roots near the surface
Turtles

***

Undergrowth
Unspoiled / Virgin

***

Vines

***

Warm
Waterfall

24 PLANTS AND TREES (SIGHT)

Abundant
Accent / accents
Ancient (hiding ancient statues or crumbling ancient cities)
Annual
Aromatic
Array
Assorted
Attention-getting
Attractive
Autumn
Awakening

***

Background
Bark
Basket
Bear flowers
Beautiful
Beauty
Bed
Bigger
Blend
Bloom
Blossom
Blush
Blushing

Bold
Boldly colored
Border
Botanic garden
Bough
Branch
Branching pattern
Breathtaking
Bright
Brilliance
Brilliant
Buckets
Bud
Budding
Bulb
Bunch
Bundle
Burst
Burst into bloom
Bush
Butterfly garden

***

Captivating
Capture
Catch the light
Charm
Charming
Cheerful
Climbing
Clusters
Color combination
Colorful
Complement
Complementary
Compost
Contrast with / Contrasting
Cover crop
Cultivate
Cutting

***

Darling
Dazzling
Debris
Decorative
Delicate
Delightful
Disease-resistant
Display
Distinctive
Divine
Dormant
Dramatic
Drill
Drought-tolerant
Dwarf

***

Easily-controlled
Eden
Edging plant
Edible
Elegant
Enchanting
Established
Ever-blooming
Exotic
Exquisite
Extravagant
Eye-catching

***

Fall
Fan (shaped)
Fanned
Fascinating
Fast-growing
Favorite
Feature
Fertilizer
Festive

Field
Fields of ___
Flair
Float
Floral
Flourish
Flower
Flowering
Focal point
Foliage
Foliage
Fragrance
Fragrant
Fresh
Freshly picked
Fruit
Fruit tree
Full/partial shade
Full/partial sun

***

Garden
Glorious
Gorgeous
Graceful
Graft / Grafting
Grass
Ground cover
Group
Grove
Grow
Growth

***

Hardy
Harvest
Healthier
Healthy
Heavenly
Heavy (with fruit or blossoms)
Herbs

Highlight
Hue
Hybrid

***

Impression
Impressive
In bloom
Intensely fragrant

***

Jewel-toned
Joyful

***

Kaleidoscope

***

Landscaping
Large
Lasting
Leaf
Leaf litter
Light
Live
Long stem
Long-lasting
Lovely
Low-growing
Luminous
Lush

***

Magical
Magnificent
Majestic
Mature
Medicinal
Medley
Mesh strainer (sap)
Mesmerizing
Mingle
Mix
Moisture

Moonlight
Morning
Mosaic
Mulch
Multicolored

***

Native
Nestled
Nightfall
Nutrients

***

Old-growth
Orchard
Orchard-fresh
Organic
Ornamental
Oversized

***

Paired
Paradise
Passionate
Pastel
Pendulous
Perennial
Petal
Petite
Plume
Pollen
Precious
Pretty
Pristine
Pruned

***

Radiant
Rainbow
Rare
Ready-to-bloom
Regal
Rich

Romantic
Rustic

**

Sap
Screen (growth acts like a living screen)
Seasonal
Seed
Seedling
Select
Sentimental
Shade
Shade plant
Shady
Shallow
Ship
Shoot
Show
Showy
Shrub
Silky
Silky-smooth
Soft
Soil
Special
Spectacular
Spray
Spread
Spring
Sprout
Statuesque
Stem
Storage container (for sap)
Striking
Strong-growing
Stunning
Sturdy
Summery
Sun
Sunburst

Sun-kissed
Sunny
Sunrise
Sunshine
Surprise
Sweet
Sweet-smelling
Symbiotic
Symphony

***

Tapping spiles/spouts (for maple sap)
Tasty
Tender
Thriving
Tolerant
Transform
Transplant
Treasure
Treasured
Tree
Tribute
Trio
Tropical-looking
Trunk
Twig

***

Unforgettable
Unique
Unusual
Upright
Useful

***

Valley
Variegated
Variety
Vibrant
Vines
Visual impact
Visually stimulating

***

Watercolor
Weed
Whimsical
Winter

***

Year-round
Yield
Young

Negative descriptions of Trees and Plants

Bruised
Bugs

***

Cheap
Common
Crabgrass
Crowded

***

Dehydrated
Die
Disease
Drab
Draught
Droop
Drooping
Dying

***

Erosion

***

Faded

***

Frost

***

Heat

***

Invasive

***

Lifeless

***

Old
Ordinary
Out of place

***

Pests
Plain
Poisonous
Problem areas

***

Rodents

***

Sag
Sagging
Scorched
Snow
Spent
Sun exposure

***

Tasteless

***

Unstable

***

Weak
Wilt
Wilted
Wither
Withered
Wrinkly

25 PLANTS AND TREES (ACTIONS)

This section contains words that a character can do to plants or trees as well as actions by trees and plants.

Absorb
Adorn

**

Bloom
Blooming
Blossoming
Boiling
Bore
Budding
Build

**

Canning (ex. Maple to make syrup)
Choose
Chop
Clip
Collect
Compost
Control
Cover
Cull
Cultivate
Cut back

***

Deplete
Detach
Display
Distill
Drain
Drill

***

Elicit
Emerge
Exhaust
Expose
Extract

***

Feed
Fertilize
Filtering
Flower

***

Gather
Germinate
Graft
Graze
Grow

***

Harvest

***

Insert

***

Juice

***

Maintain
Mature
Mow

***

Nurture

***

Pick
Plant

Plow
Pluck
Pollinate
Propagate
Prune

***

Reap
Remove
Replant (with trees)
Ripen
Root

***

Sap
Seed
Select
Serve
Shade
Single out
Sort
Sow
Stagger
Steal
Supplement

***

Tap
Tend
Thrive
Till
Tolerate
Train
Transplant
Trim

***

Use

***

Water
Weed

***

Yield

26 LEAVES AND PETALS

You can describe leaves and flowers as you (or your character) sees them. Or you can use a metaphor, simile or analogy. I would recommend looking through this list as well as the colors master list found toward the end of this book. Search for an image online then be creative in describing the scene as I did below.

My grandmother had a hibiscus bush that grew past her roof. The leaves were a deep, rich green color that covered most of its woody stem. Most of the year, the bush was covered in big, pale orange blooms with bright red stamens loaded with pollen. Of all her flowers, I admired the hibiscus the most, probably because its delicate petals reminded me of a dress, long and flowing, wispy and feminine.

LEAF SHAPE

Barbs
Blunt end

***

Circular

***

Diamond shaped (Rhomboid)

***

Fan shaped

Finger like lobes
Flaring
Flat

* * *

Grooves

* * *

Heart shaped

* * *

Indentations

* * *

Kidney shaped

* * *

Lance shaped
Lobed

* * *

Notches

* * *

Oblong
Oval

* * *

Pointed

* * *

Ridges

* * *

Shield shaped
Sickle shaped
Slender and pointed (needle like)
Smooth
Spear shaped

* * *

Tapering to a long point
Translucent
Triangular

* * *

Wave like
With holes

FLOWER SHAPE

Asymmetric

***

Bell shaped (ex. Bell flower)
Bladder shaped (bladdernut)
Butterfly shaped (Lupine)

***

Cross shaped (phlox, wallflower)
Crown shaped (ex. Daffodil, passion flower)
Cup shaped (tulips)

***

Funnel shaped (wild petunia, Virginia bluebells)

***

Hooded (Monk's hood)

***

Lip like petals (blue sage/Salvia)

***

Petals bent back (lily, shooting star)

***

Star shaped / Five petals (Jasmine, Dianthus)
Strap like (zinnia)
Symmetric

***

Tube shaped (fuchsia)
Tube with flat lobes (primrose, rhododendron)

***

Urn shaped or pitcher shaped (Grape hyacinth)

***

With a spur- nectar to attract pollinators (delphinium, columbine, nasturtium)

With extra petals (roses, amaryllis)

Describing PETALS

Broad

***

Colorful

***

Delicate
Distinct

***

Few
Folded
Fragile

***

Inner

***

Large

***

Many

***

Narrow
Numerous

***

Outer

***

Pale
Pointed

***

Scattered
Separate
Showy
Small
Soft

***

Tiny

***

United
Upper

***

Velvety

***

Withered
Wide

27 SWAMP (SIGHT)

Below are a list of things that you would see in a generic Swamp. Do your research to determine the specific plants and animal life you would find in your specific Swamp. You need to decide whether you will describe a Freshwater or a Saltwater Swamp.

Freshwater Swamps

Alligators

***

Bait
Bass
Bears (Black Bear in FL)
Bitterns
Boats
Bog
Brackish water
Bushes

***

Caiman
Carnivorous plants
Catfish
Charts
Cottonmouth
Cranes
Crayfish/ Crawfish/ crawdad / mudbug

Cypress

***

Damselfly
Dangerous or Toxic plants
Deluge
Dock
Drainage
Duckweed

***

Eastern coral snake
Eastern diamondback rattlesnake
Eerie
Eggs
Egrets

***

Fire (occasionally)
Fish
Floating platforms
Forbidding
Freshwater

***

Glade

***

Herons
Houseboats
Hummock

***

Insects
Islands

***

Lakes
Lizards
Lush

***

Mangroves
Maps
Marsh
Medicinal plants
Minks

Mire
Moist
Moor
Muck
Mucky river bottom
Mud
Muddy water (light brown; tan)

***

Nests

***

Oppressive
Overgrown

***

Panthers (Florida)
Peat bog
Poison-Ivy
Poison-sumac
Pygmy rattlesnake

***

Rat snake
River otter
Rotting

***

Sassafras
Saw palmetto
Sawgrass
Sea water
Seasonal flooding
Shelter on high ground
Shrubs
Sinister
Slow moving water / Stagnant water
Sludge
Snakes
Songbirds
Spanish moss
Streams

***

Tall grasses
Timber rattlesnake
Torrent
Tupelo trees
Turtles

***

Water
Water is reflective like a mirror
Water moccasin
Wet / Drought (depends on location/season)
Willow
Woodpecker

Saltwater Swamp

Birds
Breaker

***

Conchs
Crabs
Crest
Current

***

Eddy

***

Flood

***

High tide

***

Insects

***

Mangrove
Mud

***

Sand
Seawater
Shellfish

Spawn
Storm Surge
Swell
Swirl

***

Tall, thin roots
Tropical coastline

***

Undertow

***

Wave

28 SWAMP (ACTIONS)

This list contains action words that your Character(s) can do in a Swamp. Do not forget about the creatures (and plants) that live in the Swamp. They are just as active as your Character(s), so be sure to describe their actions as well.

Assault
Avoid

***

Bake
Bash
Bean (hit)
Beat
Bite
Blister
Boil
Bolt
Bother
Bread
Bypass

***

Camp
Canoeing
Cast (a net)
Change
Charge

Chase
Chop
Chop (down)
Cling
Clip
Clock
Club
Confront
Cook
Cope
Cruise
Cut

***

Deep Fry
Develop
Disappear
Dissolve
Disturb
Document
Dodge
Drift
Drown

***

Eat
Elude
Encounter
Endure
Eradicate
Escape
Evade
Explore

***

Fight
Filter
Fish
Flee
Float
Flood
Fluctuate

Follow
Fry

***

Grab
Grapple
Grill

***

Harm
Harvest (wood)
Heal
Hide
Hightail
Hound
Hunt

***

Infiltrate
Invade

***

Jump

***

Leave
Linger
Lose

***

Maneuver
Meddle
Meet
Molest

***

Observe
Operate (boat)
Outlive

***

Paddle
Pan fry
Persist
Photograph
Pickle
Poach (both meanings)

Pound
Practice
Protect
Punch
Pursue

***

Race
Recover
Release
Rescue
Retreat
Revive
Ride out
Roast
Row
Run

***

Saturate
Save
Scale (remove scales from fish)
Scrutinize
Season (adding flavor to food)
Seek
Serve
Shift
Shun
Simmer
Skin
Slice
Slip
Slog
Smoke (cooking and cigarettes)
Smuggle
Sneak
Snoop
Soak
Spy
Stab
Steam

Steep
Stew
Strike
Struggle with (person, animal, against nature)
Suffer
Survive
Swim

***

Trace
Trap
Turn

***

Vanish

***

Weave

29 SWAMP (TOUCH)

Broken

***

Dry (if there is a dry season)

***

Jagged

***

Leather

***

Polished

***

Raised
Ridged
Rough (bark, alligator skin)

***

Scaled
Sharp (Alligator teeth)
Sleek
Slimy (frogs)
Smooth (snake skin)
Solid
Spongy

***

Weathered
Wet
Wide

NOTE: For more TEXTURES, check out the **TEXTURE Master List** on page 257.

30 SWAMP (SOUNDS)

Air boats

***

Buzzing

***

Cawing
Chirping
Chirping of Crickets at night
Croaking

***

Deep growl (alligator)
Growl

***

Grunting
Gunshots

***

Hiss (snake or alligator)
Hooting

***

Quacks

***

Rumbling bellow (alligator)
Rustling

***

Screaming (eagle)
Songbirds singing

***

Tweeting
Twittering

***

Woodpecker drumming, hammering, pounding

NOTE: Check out the Master List of Animal Sounds on page 227.

31 SWAMP (SMELL)

Briny (saltwater marsh)

***

Dank
Death
Decay

***

Fragrant (flowers)

***

Green

***

Musk (animal)

***

Salty (saltwater marsh)

Note: For more descriptive words about Scents, check out the
SCENTS Master List on page 249.

32 SWAMP (TASTE)

When it comes to taste, usually it means you're sitting down to eat or drink. What you are eating and drinking largely depends on the specific location, time period and type of animal available. This section is thin, however, a complete list of TASTE descriptors (the **Master List of Taste)** is located toward the end of this book.

Alligator can taste like Fish / Rabbit / Chicken / Frog legs

***

Bland

***

Chewy
Crispy

***

Flaky
Fried (catfish)

***

Garlic / Garlicky

***

Lemon/ lemony
Lemony and garlicky (catfish seasoning)
Light, mild, hint of sweetness (catfish)

***

Sweet, meaty, earthy (catfish)

***

Tough

NOTE: For a complete list of TASTE descriptors, check out the **Master List of Taste** on page XX.

33 COLOR MASTER LIST

What words would you use to describe your garden at the height of spring?

Blazing with color?

Is your sick aunt's face ashen?

Does your teenager suffer from blotchy skin?

Are you wearing checkered underwear?

Did I make you look?

Did you form a mental image of checkered underwear?

That's why I created this list and why you should use this list to add a little spice to your descriptions.

Don't just think of using these words with flowers. Think above and beyond.

What if your protagonist landed in a world where the colors are all faded? Or neon bright?

Pick one of these words and pair it with any of the colors in the following section.

Ablaze
Accent
Accented
Achromatic
Ashen
Ashy
Atomic

***

Beaming
Blazing
Bleached
Bleak
Blended
Blotchy
Bold
Brash
Bright
Brightness
Brilliance
Brilliant
Burnt

***

Cast
Checkered
Chromatic
Classic
Clean
Colorant
Coloration
Colored
Colorful
Colorless
Complementing
Compound Colors
Contrasting
Cool
Coordinating
Crisp

***

Dappled
Dark
Deep
Delicate
Depth
Digital
Dim

Dimension
Dirty
Discolored
Dotted
Drab
Dreary
Dull
Dusty
Dye

***

Earth
Electric
Eye-Catching

***

Faded
Faint
Festive
Fiery
Finish
Flashy
Flattering
Flecked
Florescent
Frosty
Full-Toned

***

Glaze
Gleams
Glimmers
Glint
Glistening
Glowing
Gradation
Gradient

***

Harsh
Hazy
Hot
Hue

Hued

***

Icy
Illuminated
Incandescence
Incandescent
Intense
Interwoven
Iridescence
Iridescent

***

Kaleidoscopic

***

Lambent
Light
Lightness
Loud
Luminosity
Luminous
Luster
Lusterless
Lustrous

***

Majestic
Marbled
Matte
Medium
Mellow
Milky
Mingled
Mixed
Monochromatic
Monotone
Motley
Mottled
Muddy
Multicolored
Multi-hued
Murky

***

Natural
Neutral

***

Opacity
Opalescence
Opalescent
Opaque

***

Pale
Pastel
Patchwork
Patchy
Patterned
Perfect
Picturesque
Pigment
Pigmentation
Plain
Pop of color
Primary
Primary Color
Prismatic
Psychedelic
Pure
Purity

***

Radiance
Radiant
Rainbow
Reflective
Rich
Royal
Ruddy
Rustic

***

Satiny
Saturated
Saturation

Secondary
Shade
Shaded
Shadow
Sheen
Sheer
Shimmer
Shine
Shining
Shiny
Shocking
Showy
Smoky
Soft
Solid
Somber
Soothing
Sooty
Sparkling
Speckled
Spectrum
Stained
Streaked
Streaky
Striking
Strong Neutral
Subtle
Sunny
Swatch
Swirling

***

Tinge
Tinged
Tint
Tinted
Tonal
Tone
Toned
Traditional

Translucent
Transparent
Two-Tone

***

Undertone
Undiluted
Uneven
Uniform

***

Value
Vibrant
Vivid

***

Wan
Warm
Washed-Out
Waxen
Wild

34 COLORS (ACTIONS)

What's that you say? Colors can't do anything?
I beg to differ.
The colors on the wall can **fade** over time.
Do you have silver **highlights** in your hair? Or are you getting older like me?

Think about homes, hair, clothes, buildings, floral arrangements, every day objects.
Don't just say your newest client/blind date/in Law dresses like a clown. Describe his clothing, his color choices. Show me how the colors he chose **clashes**.

What ACTIONS can *you* do with colors?

Accent
Appear
Attract

***

Balance
Blare
Blaze
Bleach
Blend
Brighten
Bring Out

Burn

***

Captivate
Cast
Catch The Eye
Clash
Color
Combine
Complement
Contrast
Coordinate

***

Darken
Dye

***

Embellish
Emit

***

Fade
Flash
Flatter
Fleck
Flow
Flush

***

Glare
Glaze
Gleam
Glimmer
Glisten
Glow

***

Harmonize
Highlight

***

Illuminate
Infuse

***

Juxtapose

***

Light
Lighten

***

Match
Merge
Mix
Morph

***

Overlap

***

Paint
Pair With
Pop

***

Radiate
Redden
Reflect

***

Saturate
Shade
Shimmer
Shine
Smudge
Sparkle
Speckle
Spill
Stain
Stand Out
Streak
Swirl

***

Tint
Trace
Transform

***

Weave

35 BLACK

Sometimes you want to state simply that the color of something is black. In other instances, you might want to use a simile, analogy or metaphor to indicate the color of an object.

Ebony skin.
Covered in soot.
Her son looked like he had been playing in a coal mine. Alternatively, you could have the mother ask her son, "Were you playing in a coal mine?"
Smoky eye shadow.

Black
Black Cat
Black Coffee
Black Pearl
Black Pepper
Blackboard
Blackout
Blue-Black
Bow Tie

***

Carbon
Caviar
Chalkboard
Charcoal

Coal

***

Ebony
Eclipse
Eyelash

***

Fig

***

Gothic

***

Hearse

***

Ink / Inky

***

Jet Black

***

Kettle
Kohl

***

Licorice

***

Mascara
Midnight Black Or Midnight
Molasses

***

Night Sky
Ninja

***

Obsidian
Onyx
Outer Space

***

Penguin
Piano Key
Pitch Black
Pupil

***

Raven

***

Sable
Sea Lion
Shadow
Smoky
Sooty
Spade
Spider

***

Tar
Tarmac
Tuxedo

36 BLUE

Sometimes you want to state simply that the color of something is blue. In other instances, you might want to use a simile, analogy or metaphor to indicate the color of an object.

Aqua Blue
Aquamarine
Azure

***

Baby Blue
Bluebell
Blue Ice
Blue Jeans
Blueberry
Bluebird
Blue-Green

***

Cadet Blue
Caribbean Blue
Caribbean Turquoise
Cerulean
Cobalt
Cornflower
Cyan

***

Dark Blue

Dark Slate
Deep Sky Blue
Denim Blue

***

Frostbite

***

Heather

***

Icy Blue
Imperial Blue
Indigo
Inky Blue
Iridescent Blue of a peacock's feathers

***

Lapis
Lapis Lazuli
Light Blue

***

Marine
Midnight Blue

***

Navy Blue
Neon Blue
Nighttime

***

Ocean

***

Pacific
Pale Blue
Pastel Blue
Police Officer Uniform
Pool
Powder Blue
Prussian Blue

***

Ribbon
Robin Egg
Royal Blue

***

Sapphire
Sky Blue
Slate
Stained Glass
Summer Sky
Surf
Swimming Pool

***

Teal
Tiffany Blue
True Blue
Turquoise
Ultramarine
Verdigris
Violet Blue
Washed Denim

37 BROWN / TAN

Sometimes you want to state simply that the color of something is brown or tan. In other instances, you might want to use a simile, analogy or metaphor to indicate the color of an object.

Acorn
Auburn
Autumn Leaf

***

Barbecue Sauce
Bark
Bear
Beetle
Biscuit
Branch
Brick
Bronze
Brown
Brown Sugar
Brunette
Burnt Sienna (Reddish Brown)
Burnt Toast / Burned Toast
Burnt Umber
Butterscotch

***

Cafe Au Lait

Camel
Cappuccino
Caramel
Cardboard
Chestnut
Chocolate
Cinnamon
Cocoa
Coffee
Coffee Bean
Coffee Stain
Copper

***

Dark Chocolate
Dark Citrine
Deer
Desert Sand
Dirt

***

Earth
Earthenware

***

Fawn
Football
Fox
Freckle

***

Ginger
Golden Brown

***

Hazel
Henna (Can be Brown or Black)

***

Kangaroo
Khaki

Leather
Lion

***

Mahogany
Maple
Maple Sugar
Meatball
Milk Chocolate
Mink
Mocha
Mud

***

Nougat
Nude
Nut
Nutmeg

***

Oak

***

Pancake
Peanut Butter
Potato
Pretzel
Redwood
Rich Earth
Roan
Root Beer
Rosewood
Ruddy
Russet
Rust

***

Saddle
Sand
Sepia
Sienna (Yellow Brown color. When burnt, it's Burnt Sienna, which is Reddish Brown)
Sorrel (Refers to horse color - a Reddish color)
Steak

***

Tan
Tawny

Toast
Tumbleweed
Tweed

***

Walnut
Wheat
Whiskey

38 GRAY / SILVER

Sometimes you want to state simply that the color of something is gray or silver. In other instances, you might want to use a simile, analogy or metaphor to indicate the color of an object.

Ash

          ***

Battleship

          ***

Cadet
Charcoal
Chrome
Concrete
Cool Gray

          ***

Dim
Dolphin
Dove
Dusty Chalkboard

          ***

Elephant

          ***

Fog

          ***

Grandma
Granite

Gray
Gray Clouds
Grey
Gunmetal

***

Haze
Hippopotamus

***

Koala

***

Metal
Mist
Mouse

***

Overcast
Owl
Oyster

***

Pewter
Pigeon
Platinum

***

Rainy Day
Rhinoceros
River Rock

***

Salt And Pepper
Sardine
Seal
Shark
Silver
Slate
Smoke
Soot
Steel
Stone
Storm
Stormy Sea

***

Taupe
Thunder Cloud

***

Warm Gray
Wet Sidewalk
Wool

***

Zinc

Taupe
Thunder Cloud

***

Warm Gray
Wet Sidewalk
Wool

***

Zinc

39 GREEN

Sometimes you want to state simply that the color of something is green. In other instances, you might want to use a simile, analogy or metaphor to indicate the color of an object.

Absinthe
Algae
Alligator
Apple
Aqua
Army Fatigues
Artichoke
Asparagus
Avocado

***

Bay Leaf
Bluegrass
Boxwood
Broccoli

***

Cabbage
Cactus
Caterpillar
Celery
Chartreuse
Chive

Chlorophyll
Clover
Crocodile
Cucumber
Cyan
Cypress

         ***

Dark Khaki
Dark Olive
Dollar Bill
Drab Olive

         ***

Eel
Emerald
Evergreen
Fern
Forest
Frog

         ***

Granny Smith Apple
Grass
Grasshopper
Green Apple
Green Olive
Green Pepper
Green Tea
Green-Yellow

         ***

Holly
Honeydew
Hunter Green
Iceberg Lettuce
Iguana
Ivy

         ***

Jade
Jungle

         ***

Kelp

Kermit
Key Lime

***

Leaf
Leprechaun
Lettuce
Lichen
Light Cyan
Lime Green
Lizard

***

Melon Rind
Metallic Mint
Mint
Moss
Myrtle

***

Neon Green

***

Olive Drab
Olive Green

***

Parrot
Pea
Pea Soup
Pear
Pickle
Pine
Pistachio

***

Sage
Sea
Sea foam
Seaweed
Shamrock
Spinach
Spring
Spring Bud
Sprout

Spruce
Summer Grass
Swamp

***

Turtle

***

Verdant
Verdigris

***

Wasabi

***

Zucchini

40 ORANGE / GOLD

    Sometimes you want to state simply that the color of something is orange or golden. In other instances, you might want to use a simile, analogy or metaphor to indicate the color of an object.

10-Karat Gold
24-Karat Gold

***

Amber
Apricot

***

Basketball
Blood Orange
Bourbon
Burnt Orange

***

Candlelight
Candy Corn
Cantaloupe
Carnelian
Carotene
Carrot Orange
Cheddar
Cinnamon
Copper

Copper Penny
Coral

***

Dark Orange
Dark Salmon
Dayglo Orange

***

Embers

***

Fall Leaves
Flame

***

Ginger
Gold
Golden
Goldfish

***

Light Orange
Light Salmon

***

Mandarin (Orange)
Mango
Marigold
Melon
Monarch Butterfly

***

Neon Orange

***

Old Gold
Orange
Orange Ice Pop
Orange Juice
Orange Peel
Orange Sherbet
Orange Soda
Orange-Red

***

Papaya
Peach

Persimmon
Pumpkin

***

Russet
Rust

***

Safety Vest
Saffron
Salamander
Starfish
Sunrise

***

Tabby
Tangelo
Tangerine
Tawny
Tiger Orange
Tiger Stripe
Traffic Cone

***

Yam

41 PINK

Sometimes you want to state simply that the color of something is pink. In other instances, you might want to use a simile, analogy or metaphor to indicate the color of an object.

Amaranth
Apricot
Ash Rose

***

Baby
Baby Cheeks
Bacon
Ballerina
Ballet
Ballet Slipper
Begonia
Blush
Bougainvillea
Bubblegum

***

Cadillac
Cameo
Carmine
Carnation
Cerise
Champagne

Cheeks
Cherry Blossom
Conch
Coral
Cotton Candy
Cranberry
Cupcake

***

Dusty Rose

***

Eraser

***

Flamingo
Flesh
Flesh-Colored
Fuchsia

***

Grapefruit

***

Hibiscus
Hot Pink

***

Jellyfish

***

Lavender
Light Plum
Lipstick

***

Magenta
Misty Rose
Mulberry

***

Neon

***

Orchid

***

Pale
Pastel
Peach

Peach Puff
Peony
Persian Rose
Petunia
Pig
Pink Diamond
Pink Grapefruit
Pink Lemonade
Pink Sherbet
Polka Dot
Powder

***

Raspberry
Rose
Rose Petal
Rose Quartz

***

Sand
Seashell
Shocking
Soft
Strawberry Jam
Strawberry Milkshake
Sunset

***

Tea Rose
Thistle
Tongue
Tulip
Turnip

***

Worm

42 PURPLE

Sometimes you want to state simply that the color of something is purple. In other instances, you might want to use a simile, analogy or metaphor to indicate the color of an object.

Amethyst
Aubergine

***

Beet
Bilberry
Blackberry
Blackcurrant
Blue Violet
Blueberry
Brandywine
Bruise
Byzantium

***

Cabbage
Cerise
Claret
Concord Grape
Currant

***

Dahlia
Dark Orchid

Dark Raspberry
Dark Violet

***

Eggplant

***

Fandango

***

Grape
Grape Jam
Grape Jelly

***

Heliotrope
Hyacinth

***

Inky
Iris

***

Juice

***

Lavender
Lavender Blush
Lilac
Lollipop

***

Magenta
Mauve
Monster
Mulberry

***

Opal
Orchid

***

Pale Plum
Pansy
Passion fruit
Pastel
Periwinkle
Plum
Prune

***

Quartz

***

Raisin
Raspberry
Red Onion
Rhubarb
Royal

***

Thistle
True
Turnip

***

Violet
Violet Red

***

Wild Berry
Wild Grape
Wine
Wisteria

43 RED

Sometimes you want to state simply that the color of something is red. In other instances, you might want to use a simile, analogy or metaphor to indicate the color of an object.

Alizarin Crimson
Amaranth
Apple
Auburn
Autumn Leaf

***

Barn
Beet
Blood
Blush
Bordeaux
Bougainvillea
Bourbon
Brick
Bright Red
Burgundy
Burnt Sienna

***

Candy Apple
Cardinal
Carmine

Carnelian
Cerise
Cherry
Chestnut
Chili Pepper Red
Cinnabar
Claret
Copper
Coral
Crab
Cranberry
Crimson

***

Dark Cerise
Dark Red
Deep Pink
Devil

***

Faded Rose
Fire
Fire Engine
Fire Truck
Flame
Fruit Punch

***

Garnet
Geranium

***

Hibiscus
Hot Pink

***

Ketchup

***

Ladybug
Lipstick
Lobster

***

Magenta
Magma

Maroon

***

Nose

***

Orange-Red

***

Paprika
Pepperoni
Persimmon
Pink Red
Pomegranate
Poppy

***

Rabbit Eye
Radish
Rare Steak
Raspberry
Red
Red Carpet
Red Licorice
Red Pepper
Red Potato
Red Velvet
Red Velvet Cake
Red Wine Vinegar
Rose
Rosewood
Rouge
Ruby Red
Russet
Rust

***

Sangria
Scarlet
Sports Car
Stop Light
Stop Sign
Strawberry

***

Tawny
Tawny Port
Terracotta / Terra Cotta
Tomato
Tomato Bisque
Torch

***

Vermilion

***

Watermelon Flesh
Wine
Winter Apple

44 WHITE

Sometimes you want to state simply that the color of something is white. In other instances, you might want to use a simile, analogy or metaphor to indicate the color of an object.

Alabaster
Albino
Antique
Arctic
Argent
Ashen

***

Beige
Birch
Biscuit
Bisque
Blanched
Blanched Almond
Bleached
Blonde
Bone
Buff

***

Camel
Canvas Beige
Chalk

Coconut
Contrast
Cotton
Cream

***

Diamond
Dove

***

Ecru
Eggshell

***

Flax
Flour
Fog
French Beige
Frosted

***

Ghost
Goose

***

Hemp

***

Ivory

***

Lace
Latte
Light Tan
Lily / Lily white
Linen

***

Marshmallow
Milk
Mother-Of-Pearl
Mushroom

***

Neutral
Nude

***

Oatmeal

Off-white
Old Lace
Opal

***

Paper
Pearl
Piano Key
Polar
Porcelain
Powder
Pure

***

Raw Cotton

***

Sand
Sandstone
Seashell
Sheep
Sheet
Shell
Shining Star
Silvery
Smoky Beige
Snow
Solid
Spotless
Sugar

***

Toothpaste

***

Vanilla

***

Waxen
Wedding
Whey
White Chocolate
White Smoke
Winter Snow

45 YELLOW

Sometimes you want to state simply that the color of something is yellow. In other instances, you might want to use a simile, analogy or metaphor to indicate the color of an object.

Banana
Bleached Blond
Blond / Blonde
Buff
Bumblebee
Butter
Buttercup
Butternut Squash
Butterscotch

***

Cadmium
Canary
Champagne
Chardonnay
Citrine
Corn
Corn silk
Cream
Custard

***

Daffodil

Dandelion
Duckling

***

Egg Yolk
Electric

***

Flax
Flesh Tone
French Fry

***

Gold
Golden
Golden Bronze
Goldenrod

***

Highlighter
Honey

***

Lemon
Lemon Chiffon
Lemon Drop
Lemon Meringue
Lemon Peel
Lemon Sherbet
Linen
Lion

***

Maize
Marigold
Mellow
Metallic Gold
Mimosa
Mustard

***

Ochre
Olive
Omelette

***

Palomino

Papaya
Parakeet
Pencil
Peroxide Blond / Blonde
Pineapple
Popcorn

***

Raincoat

***

Saffron
School Bus
Squash
Straw
Sunflower
Sun glow
Sunset
Sunshine

***

Taxi Cab
Titanium
Topaz (Comes in various colors)

***

Vanilla

***

Wheat

***

Yolk

46 ACTIONS MASTER LIST

Abandon
Abduct
Abolish
Absorb
Abstain
Abuse
Acquire
Add
Advance
Agitate (mix or bother)
Analyze
Annihilate
Annoy
Apprehend
Arch / arched (arch your back or a plant forms an arch)
Argue
Arrest
Ascend
Asphyxiate
Assassinate
Assault
Avoid

***

Backpacking
Badger

Bag (as in capture)
Bake
Bash
Bean (hit)
Beat
Beguile
Belay/ Belaying (climbing technique)
Berate
Beset
Besiege
Bet
Bewitch
Bind
Bite
Blackmail
Blister
Blocked
Boil
Bolt
Bombard
Boot
Bop
Bore
Bother
Box in
Brain (as in hit)
Bread
Break up
Bruise
Brush
Bug (as in annoy, bother)
Bully
Burn
Burrow
Burst
Bury
Bushwhacking (may carry a negative connotation)
Bypass

***

Cajole
Camp
Cancel
Cane (to beat)
Canoeing
Captivate
Capture
Careen
Caress
Carry / Carry off
Carve / Carve out
Cast (a net)
Castigate
Catch
Censure
Change
Charge (attack, as well as spending)
Charm
Chase
Cheat
Cheat (adultery)
Cheer
Choke
Choked
Chomp
Chop
Chop (down)
Clamber
Clamp
Clasp
Clean
Clean (up, off)
Climb
Clinch
Cling
Clip
Cloaked
Clobber
Clock

Close
Club
Club (as in hit)
Clutch
Coddle
Coerce
Collide
Condemn
Confront
Conquer
Constrain
Consume
Continue
Cook
Cope
Corner
Corral (gather)
Counter
Cover up
Covered
Crack
Crack up (make laugh)
Cram
Crawl
Crept
Criticize
Cross
Cross over
Crouch
Crucify
Cruise
Crush
Cuddle
Curse (put a curse on / hex / say bad words)
Cut

***

Dance / Danced
Dazzle
Decoy (act as a decoy)

Deep Fry
Defeat
Defraud
Denigrate
Descend
Despoil
Destroy
Develop
Devour
Dig
Digest
Dine
Disappear
Discover
Dismantle
Dispatch
Dissolve
Disturb
Ditch (as in drop or get rid of)
Divert
Document
Dodge
Draw
Drift
Drive
Drop
Drown
Dump

***

Earn
Eat
Electrocute
Elude
Embarrass
Embezzle
Embrace
Empty
Encounter
End (as in kill)

Endure
Enslave
Ensnare
Enter
Enthrall
Eradicate
Erase
Erupted
Escape
Evade
Examine
Excavate
Execute
Exhume
Explore
Exterminate

***

Fall
Falter
Fasten
Fear
Feast upon
Feed
Fight
Filter
Find
Finish
Finish
Fish
Fishing
Flay
Flee
Float
Floated
Flood
Flounder
Fluctuate
Flush
Fluttered

Follow
Fondle
Forage
Force
Forget
Forgive
Fry

***

Garrote
Gather
Get
Give birth
Give up
Gloat
Gnaw
Go down
Go into
Goad
Gobble
Gorge
Gouge
Grab
Grapple
Grasped
Gratify
Graze
Graze
Grieve
Grill
Guard
Guillotine
Gulp
Guzzle

***

Handle
Harass
Harm
Harvest (wood)
Hassle

Haul / Haul in
Heal
Heckle
Hesitate
Hex
Hide
Hightail
Hijack
Hike
Hinder
Hold
Hollow (out)
Hook
Hop
Hopped
Horseback Riding
Hound
Hug
Hung / Hang
Hunt
Hurt
Hypnotize

***

Ignore
Imbibe
Impede
Impugn
Infiltrate
Ingest
Inhale
Inspect
Insult
Intrigue
Invade
Investigate
Irritate
Itch

***

Jab
Jerk
Judge
Jump

***

Keep
Keep Watch
Kick
Kidnap
Kill
Kiss
Knock out
Knotted

***

Labor
Lacerate
Lash
Lay siege
Leave
Leave
Level (make even, as in construction)
Lie
Lift
Limp
Linger
Liquidate
Lit
Lock
Look into
Lose
Lower
Lumber
Lurch
Lurk
Lynch

***

Magnetize (think fantasy / paranormal / superhero special powers / building a trap or solving a problem / teaching about magnets

Maim
Malign
Maltreat
Maneuver
March
Massacre
Massage
Masticate
Masturbate
Maul
Meddle
Meet
Mesmerize
Mine
Mining
Misjudge
Miss
Mistreat
Molest
Mug
Munch
Murder
Nab
Nag
Nail (as in catch or attaching to something)
Nap
Needle (as in bother)
Neglect
Negotiate
Neutralize (as in kill)
Nibble
Nip
Nix
Note
Notice

Nudge
Nullify
Nurse (feeding baby or nurse back to health)

***

Obliterate
Obscure
Observe
Obtain
Occupy
Open
Operate (boat/ surgery)
Outlive
Outrun
Outshine
Overcome
Overlook
Overtake
Overthrow

***

Paddle
Pan fry
Panic
Pass over
Pass through
Pat
Patrol
Peer into
Pelt (as in throw)
Penetrate
Perch
Persecute
Persist
Pester
Pet
Photograph
Pick
Pick (fruit)
Pick on
Pickle

Pierce
Pilfer
Pillage
Pinch
Pitch
Plan
Plant
Plead
Pluck
Pluck (berries, fruits)
Plunder
Poach (both meanings)
Poison
Pound
Practice
Prevent
Probe
Procure
Prod
Prohibit
Protect
Provoke
Pry
Pull
Pulverize
Pummel
Punch
Punish
Purloin
Pursue
Push
Put to death

***

Race
Raid
Ramble
Ransack
Ransom
Rape

Ravage
Reach
Reap
Recall
Recover
Reel
Relax
Release
Remember
Remove
Rend
Repeal
Rescind
Rescue
Resolve
Retreat
Reveal
Revel
Revive
Revoke
Ride (as in bother)
Ride out
Rifle (through)
Roam
Roast
Rob
Rock climbing
Roost
Root (out)
Rose
Row
Rub
Ruin
Ruminate
Run
Rush (as in charging at something / someone)

***

Sack (as in fire)
Sacrifice
Saturate
Save
Scale
Scale (remove scales from fish)
Scamper
Scare
Scarf (as in eat, scarf down)
Scold
Scoop (out)
Score
Scout
Scramble
Scrape
Scratch
Scratched
Scrub
Scrutinize
Seal
Search
Season (adding flavor to food)
Secure
Secure (to make safe)
Seduce
See through
Seek
Seize
Separate
Serve
Set aside
Sever
Shake
Share
Shave
Shield
Shift
Shook

Shoplift
Shout
Shove
Shovel
Shrouded
Shun
Seize
Sift
Simmer
Skim
Skin
Slam
Slap
Slash
Slash
Slaughter
Slave
Slay
Sleep
Slice
Slide
Slink
Slip
Slog
Slug
Slump
Smack
Smash
Smoke (cooking and cigarettes)
Smother
Smuggle
Snack
Snag
Snap
Snatch
Sneak
Snitch
Snoop
Snuff (as in kill)

Snuggle
Soak
Soak (hot springs)
Sock (as in hit)
Solve
Spank
Spit (on)
Spite
Splash
Spot
Spread
Spy
Squash
Squeeze
Squelch
Stab
Stab
Stash
Steal
Steam
Steep
Stew
Stick up (for or rob)
Stir
Stomp
Stood
Stoop
Stop
Store
Storm (the castle)
Strangled
Stretched
Strike
Strip
Stroke
Stroll
Struggle with (person, animal, against nature)
Study
Stuff

Stumble
Suffer
Suffocate
Sup
Support
Surrender
Survey
Survive
Swallow
Swat
Swayed
Sweat
Sweep
Swim
Swindle
Swing
Swipe
Switch

***

Take
Tangled
Tantalize
Taunt
Tear down
Tease
Terminate
Test
Test
Think
Threaten
Tickle
Tie
Till
Tilt
Topple
Torment
Torpedo
Torture
Tossed

Tour
Trace
Tramping
Transcend
Transport
Trap
Trapped
Trash (as in destroy)
Traverse
Trekking
Trespass
Trick
Trip (as in fall)
Trounce
Trust
Try
Tunnel
Turn
Turn over
Twisted

***

Uncover
Undo
Unearth
Use up / finish

***

Vacate
Vanish
Vanquish
Violate
Void
Vote
Vow

***

Walk
Wallop
Wander
Warp
Watch

Waver
Wax (car, body hair, surfboard)
Waylay
Weave
Whip
Whisper
Win
Wipe
Wipe out
Withdraw
Wolf (as in eat)
Wound
Wriggled
Writhed

***

Zap

47 ACTION MASTER LIST-VILLAINS

Abandon
Abduct
Abolish
Absorb
Abuse
Acquire
Advance
Agitate (mix or bother)
Annihilate
Annoy
Apprehend
Argue
Arrest
Ascend
Asphyxiate
Assassinate
Assault
Avoid

***

Badger
Bag (as in capture)
Bake
Bash
Bean (hit)
Beat

Beguile
Belay/ Belaying (climbing technique)
Berate
Beset
Besiege
Bet
Bewitch
Bind
Bite
Blackmail
Blister
Blocked
Boil
Bolt
Bombard
Boot
Bop
Bore
Bother
Box in
Brain (as in hit)
Break up
Bruise
Brush
Bug (as in annoy, bother)
Bully
Burn
Burst
Bury
Bypass

***

Cajole
Cancel
Cane (to beat)
Captivate
Capture
Carry / Carry off
Carve / Carve out
Cast (a net)

Castigate
Catch
Censure
Change
Charge (attack, as well as spending)
Charm
Chase
Cheat
Cheat (adultery)
Choke
Chomp
Chop
Chop (down)
Clamp
Clasp
Climb
Clinch
Cling
Clip
Cloaked
Clobber
Clock
Close
Club
Club (as in hit)
Clutch
Coddle
Coerce
Collide
Condemn
Confront
Conquer
Constrain
Consume
Continue
Cook
Cope
Corner
Corral (gather)

Counter
Cover up
Covered
Crack
Cram
Crept
Criticize
Cross
Cross over
Crouch
Crucify
Cruise
Crush
Cuddle (can be used to make your villain sympathetic)
Curse (put a curse on / hex / say bad words)
Cut

***

Dazzle
Deep Fry
Defeat
Defraud
Denigrate
Descend
Despoil
Destroy
Devour
Dig
Digest
Dine
Disappear
Discover
Dismantle
Dispatch
Dissolve
Disturb
Ditch (as in drop or get rid of)
Divert
Dodge
Draw

Drift
Drive
Drop
Drown
Dump

***

Eat
Electrocute
Elude
Embarrass
Embezzle
Embrace
Empty
Encounter
End (as in kill)
Endure
Enslave
Ensnare
Enter
Enthrall
Eradicate
Erase
Erupted
Escape
Evade
Examine
Excavate
Execute
Exhume
Explore
Exterminate

***

Fasten
Fear
Feast upon
Feed
Fight
Filter
Find

Finish
Fish (for information)
Flay
Flee
Float
Flood
Flush
Fluttered
Follow
Fondle
Forage
Force
Forget
Fry

***

Garrote
Gather
Get
Give birth (why not?)
Give up
Gloat
Gnaw
Go down
Go into
Goad
Gobble
Gorge
Gouge
Grab
Grapple
Grasped
Gratify
Graze
Grieve
Grill
Guard
Guillotine
Gulp
Guzzle

***

Handle
Harass
Harm
Harvest (wood)
Hassle
Haul / Haul in
Heal
Heckle
Hex
Hide
Hightail
Hijack
Hike
Hinder
Hold
Hollow (out)
Hook
Hop
Hopped
Horseback Riding
Hound
Hug
Hung / Hang
Hunt
Hurt
Hypnotize

***

Ignore
Imbibe
Impede
Impugn
Ingest
Inhale
Inspect
Insult
Intrigue
Invade
Investigate

Irritate
Itch

***

Jab
Jerk
Judge
Jump

***

Keep
Keep Watch
Kick
Kidnap
Kill
Kiss (possibly)
Knock out
Knotted

***

Labor
Lacerate
Lash
Lay siege
Leave
Level (make even, as in construction)
Lie
Lift
Limp
Liquidate
Lock
Look into
Lose
Lower
Lumber
Lurch
Lurk
Lynch

***

Magnetize (think fantasy / paranormal / superhero special powers / building a trap or solving a problem or teaching about magnets

Maim
Malign
Maltreat
Maneuver
March
Massacre
Massage
Masticate
Masturbate
Maul
Meddle
Meet
Mesmerize
Mine
Mining
Misjudge
Miss
Mistreat
Molest
Mug
Munch
Murder

***

Nab
Nag
Nail (as in catch or attaching to something)
Nap
Needle (as in bother)
Neglect
Negotiate
Neutralize (as in kill)
Nibble
Nip
Nix
Note
Notice
Nudge
Nullify
Nurse (feeding baby or nurse back to health)

***

Obliterate
Obscure
Observe
Obtain
Occupy
Open
Operate (boat)
Outlive
Outrun
Outshine
Overcome
Overlook
Overtake
Overthrow

***

Paddle
Pan fry
Panic
Pass over
Pass through
Pat
Patrol
Peer into
Pelt (as in throw)
Penetrate
Perch
Persecute
Persist
Pester
Pet
Photograph
Pick
Pick on
Pickle
Pierce
Pilfer
Pillage
Pinch

Pitch
Plan
Plant
Plead
Pluck
Pluck (berries, fruits)
Plunder
Poach (both meanings)
Poison
Pound
Practice
Prevent
Probe
Procure
Prod
Prohibit
Protect
Provoke
Pry
Pull
Pulverize
Pummel
Punch
Punish
Purloin
Pursue
Push
Put to death

***

Race
Raid
Ramble
Ransack
Ransom
Rape
Ravage
Reach
Reap
Recall

Recover
Reel
Relax
Release
Remember
Remove
Rend
Repeal
Rescind
Resolve
Retreat
Reveal
Revel
Revive
Revoke
Ride (as in bother)
Ride out
Rifle (through)
Roam
Roast
Rob
Rock climbing
Roost
Root (out)
Rose
Row
Rub
Ruin
Ruminate
Run
Rush (as in charging at something / someone)

***

Sack (as in fire)
Sacrifice
Saturate
Scale
Scale (remove scales from fish)
Scamper
Scare

Scarf (as in eat, scarf down)
Scold
Scoop (out)
Score
Scout
Scramble
Scrape
Scratch
Scratched
Scrub
Scrutinize
Seal
Search
Season (adding flavor to food)
Secure
Secure (to make safe)
Seduce
See through
Seek
Seize
Separate
Serve
Set aside
Sever
Shake
Shave
Shield
Shift
Shook
Shoplift
Shout
Shove
Shovel
Shrouded
Shun
Seize
Sift
Simmer
Skim

Skin
Slam
Slap
Slash
Slaughter
Slave
Slay
Sleep
Slice
Slide
Slink
Slip
Slog
Slug
Slump
Smack
Smash
Smoke (cooking and cigarettes)
Smother
Smuggle
Snack
Snag
Snap
Snatch
Sneak
Snitch
Snoop
Snuff (as in kill)
Soak
Soak (hot springs)
Sock (as in hit)
Solve
Spank
Spit (on)
Spite
Splash
Spot
Spread
Spy

Squash
Squeeze
Squelch
Stab
Stash
Steal
Steam
Steep
Stew
Stick up (rob)
Stir
Stomp
Stood
Stoop
Stop
Store
Storm (the castle)
Strangled
Stretched
Strike
Strip
Stroke
Stroll
Struggle with (person, animal, against nature)
Study
Stuff
Stumble
Suffer
Suffocate
Sup
Support
Surrender
Survey
Survive
Swallow
Swat
Swayed
Sweat
Sweep

Swim
Swindle
Swing
Swipe
Switch

***

Take
Tangled
Tantalize
Taunt
Tear down
Tease
Terminate
Test
Think
Threaten
Tie
Tilt
Topple
Torment
Torpedo
Torture
Tossed
Tour
Trace
Tramping
Transport
Trap
Trash (as in destroy)
Traverse
Trekking
Trespass
Trick
Trip (as in fall)
Trounce
Trust
Try
Tunnel
Turn

Turn over
Twisted

**

Uncover
Undo
Unearth
Use up / finish

**

Vacate
Vanish
Vanquish
Violate
Void
Vow

**

Walk
Wallop
Wander
Warp
Watch
Waver
Wax (car, body hair, surfboard)
Waylay
Weave
Whip
Whisper
Win
Wipe
Wipe out
Withdraw
Wolf (as in eat)
Wound

**

Zap

48 (PLEASANT) TASTE MASTER LIST

Acidic
Acrid
Aftertaste
Aged
Alligator can taste like Fish / Rabbit / Chicken / Frog legs
Alluring
Amazing
Appealing
Appetizing
Apple

***

Balanced
Balsamic
Balsamic and sweet
Bitter
Bitter almonds
Bittersweet
Bland
Blueberry
Brimming
Briny
Burnt (cooked food)
Buttery

***

Cheesy
Cherry flavored
Chewy
Chocolaty
Cinnamon
Citrus (be specific: lemony, lime, orange, grapefruit)
Clean
Cold
Comforting (pair this with comfort foods and add the scents
of comfort food ex. mashed potatoes or curry)
Complex
Cool
Coppery
Cotton candy
Cough Syrup
Creamy
Crisp
Crispy
Crumbly
Crunchy

***

Delectable
Delicate
Delicious
Delightful
Different
Distinct
Distinctive
Divine
Doughy
Dry (overcooked food)
Dry and woody

***

Earthy
Edible
Eggy
Elusive
Enjoyable

Enticing
Excellent
Exotic
Exquisite
Extraordinary
Faint
Faintest
Familiar
Fanciful
Fantastic
Fatty
Festive
Fiery
Finely textured
Finger licking
Firm
Fishy
Flaky
Flat
Flavorful
Fleshy
Floral
Fragrant
Fresh
Fresh squeezed
Freshly harvested
Freshly plucked
Fresh-picked
Fried
Fried (catfish)
Fruit-filled
Fruity
Full
Full-bodied

***

Gamy
Garden-fresh
Garlic / Garlicky
Garlicky

Gelatinous
Ginger
Gingery
Glazed
Good
Gooey
Grainy
Green
Gritty

***

Hand-picked
Harmonious
Heady
Healthy
Hearty
Heavenly
Heavy
Herbaceous
Herbal
Hot
Hungry / Hunger

***

Icy
Immune-boosting
Infused
Intense

***

Jasmine
Jolt
Juiciest
Juicy
Jumbo

***

Kick

***

Large
Lasting
Lavender (tea)
Layered

Lean
Lemon / Lemony
Lemony and garlicky (catfish seasoning)
Light
Light, mild, hint of sweetness (catfish)
Lingering (aftertaste)
Lip smacking
Little
Loaded with
Local
Locally grown
Long
Luscious

***

Malty
Market-fresh
Marvelous
Mashed
Meaty
Mellow
Melt-in-your-mouth
Memorable
Metallic
Mild
Minty
Mixed
Moist (perfectly cooked food)
Mouthwatering
Multi-layered
Mushy
Naked
Natural
Nourishing
Nutritious
Nutty

***

Oily
Old
Onion

Opulent
Orange
Orchard-fresh
Organic
Overflowing
Overpowering
Overripe
Oversized
Overwhelming (pick a specific flavor)

***

Parched
Particular
Pasty
Peach
Peak-harvested
Peculiar
Peculiar
Peeled
Peppery
Pickled
Plain
Pleasant
Pleasing
Plucked
Plump
Plush
Powdery
Powerful
Premier
Premium
Preservative-free
Pronounced
Pulp-free
Pulpy
Punch
Pure

***

Ranch (flavor)
Raw

Ready-to-eat
Refreshing
Regional
Relish
Rich
Ripe
Ripened
Roasted
Robust
Rose
Rosemary
Rotten
Rubbery
Runny

***

Sage
Salty
Satin-smooth
Satisfying
Sauteed
Savory
Scrumptious
Seared
Seasonal
Seasoned
Seductive
Seeded
Seedless
Select
Sharp
Silky
Skinned
Sleek
Slight
Slimy
Small
Smoky
Smooth
Smothered

Soft
Soggy
Solid
Soothing
Soupy
Sour
Spicy
Spoiled
Spongy
Sticky
Sticky-sweet
Sting
Strange
Strawberry
Stringy
Strong
Substantial
Subtle
Succulent
Sugary
Sunny
Superb
Superior
Supple
Sweet
Sweet and Sour (Pineapple is the main ingredient)
Sweet, meaty, earthy (catfish)
Sweetest
Syrupy

***

Tangy
Tantalizing
Tart
Tasteless
Tasty
Telltale
Tempting
Tender
Terrific

The season's best
Thick
Thirsty
Toasted
Top-quality
Tough
Tropical

***

Unfamiliar
Unique
Unmistakable

***

Vanilla
Vegan
Vegetarian
Veggie
Velvety
Vine-fresh
Vinegary
Vine-ripened
Viscous
Vitamin-infused
Vitamin-rich

***

Wallop
Warm
Washed
Watermelon
Watery
Well-balanced
Whipped
Wholesome
Wild
Wonderful
Woodsy
Woody
Yeasty
Young
Yummy

***

Zest
Zesty
Zing

49 (UNPLEASANT) TASTE MASTER LIST

Acidic
Aftertaste
Awful

***

Base
Bland
Burnt

***

Caustic
Chalky
Cough syrup
Crusty
Curdled

***

Dirty
Disagreeable
Disgusting
Doughy
Dry

***

Fatty
Fermented / Fermenting
Fetid
Fishy (can be good or bad)
Flat

Foul
Foul
Fusty

***

Gamy (can be good or bad)
Garlicky (if overpowering or the MC is a Vampire…)
Gelatinous (depends on context)
Gooey
Gritty
Grody
Gross

***

Harsh

***

Iron

***

Lousy

***

Medicinal
Metallic
Moldy
Mushy (good for babies, not for most people)
Musty
Nauseating

***

Off
Offensive
Old
Overripe

***

Peculiar
Peppery
Putrid

***

Rancid
Rank
Repellent
Repugnant
Repulsive

Revolting
Ripe
Rotten

***

Sour
Soured
Spoiled
Stagnant
Stale

***

Tainted
Tasteless
Tinny
Tough

***

Unpleasant

***

Vile
Vinegary

50 ANIMAL SOUNDS MASTER LIST

Arf

***

Baa
Bark
Bawl
Bay
Bellow
Bleat (calves, lambs)
Boom
Bow-wow
Bray
Bugle (Elk)
Buzz

***

Cackle
Caw
Chatter
Cheep
Chirp
Click (dolphin)
Cluck
Coo
Creak
Croak
Crow

Cry

***

Drum, pound, rap (woodpecker)

***

Gobble gobble (turkey)
Groan (walrus)
Growl
Grrr
Grunt
Hee-haw
Hiss
Honk
Hoo Hoo (owl)
Howl
Hum

***

Laugh (kookaburra)

***

Meow
Mew
Moo

***

Neigh
Nicker

***

Oink

***

Purr

***

Quack

***

Rat-a-tat
Ribbit
Roar
Ruff

***

Scream (eagle)
Screech
Simper

Sing
Sing (Whales, birds)
Snort
Squawk
Squeak
Squeal

***

Trill
Trumpeting (elephant)
Tweet
Twitter

***

Wail
Warble
Whine
Whinny
Whistle
Whoop
Woof (dog or wolf)

***

Yap
Yip
Yowl

51 FIRE MASTER LIST

Ash

***

Beam
Blaze
Blazing
Bonfire
Burning
Burnt / Burned
Burst Out

***

Campfire
Charring
Cinder
Coals
Combustion
Conflagration
Crackling

***

Devouring
Element
Embers
Emblazoned
Explode

***

Flame

Flare
Flash
Flicker
Fuel
Fumes

***

Glare
Gleam
Glow

***

Hearth
Heat

***

Ignite
Illuminate
Incandescence
Inferno

***

Jet

***

Lava
Light
Livid
Luminosity

***

Oxidation

***

Pop
Pyre

***

Radiate
Red Hot

***

Scalding
Scintillate
Scorching
Searing
Shimmer
Shine

Smoke
Sparkle
Sparks

***

Tinder

***

Volcanic

***

Warmth
Wood

52 PLANTS AND TREES MASTER LIST

This list contains all the words that pertain to plants and trees. If you are writing about a lawn or backyard, this list may be more helpful than the chapter on Forest.

Abloom
Absorb
Abundant
Accent / accents
Accent plant
Adorn
Ancient (hiding ancient statues or crumbling ancient cities)
Annual
Arboretum
Aromatic
Arrange
Arrangement
Array
Artful
Artfully arranged
Artistic
Assorted
Attention-getting
Attractive
Autumn
Awakening

***

Background
Bark
Basket
Bear flowers
Beautiful
Beauty
Bed
Bigger
Blend
Bloom
Blooming
Blossom
Blossoming
Blush
Blushing
Boiling
Bold
Boldly colored
Border
Bore
Botanic garden
Bough
Bouquet
Boutonniere
Branch
Branching pattern
Breathtaking
Bright
Brilliance
Brilliant
Bruised
Buckets
Bud
Budding
Bugs
Build
Bulb
Bunch

Bundle
Burst
Burst into bloom
Bush
Butterfly garden

***

Canning (ex. Maple to make syrup)
Captivating
Capture
Catch the light
Centerpiece
Charm
Charming
Cheap
Cheerful
Cherish
Choose
Chop
Classic
Climbing
Clip
Cluster
Clusters
Collecting
Collection
Color combination
Color-coordinated
Colorful
Common
Complement
Complementary
Compost
Compost
Conservatory
Container
Container garden
Container-grown
Contrast with / Contrasting
Control

Coordinate
Corsage
Country
Cover
Cover crop
Crabgrass
Create
Creative
Crowded
Cull
Cultivate
Cut back
Cutting

***

Darling
Dazzling
Debris
Decorative
Deer-resistant
Dehydrated
Delicate
Delightful
Deplete
Designed
Detach
Die
Disease
Disease-resistant
Display
Display
Distill
Distinctive
Divine
Dormant
Dozen
Drab
Drain
Dramatic
Draught

Drill
Droop
Drooping
Drought-tolerant
Dwarf
Dying

***

Easily-controlled
Easy-to-care-for
Eden
Edging plant
Edible
Elegant
Elicit
Embellish
Emerge
Enchanting
Erosion
Established
Ever-blooming
Exhaust
Exotic
Expose
Exquisite
Extract
Extravagant
Eye-catching

***

Faded
Fall
Fan (shaped)
Fanned
Fascinating
Fast-growing
Favorite
Feature
Feed
Fertilize
Fertilizer

Festive
Field
Fields of ___
Filtering
Flair
Float
Floral
Florist
Flourish
Flower
Flower arrangement
Flower shop
Flowering
Focal point
Foliage
Fragrance
Fragrant
Fresh
Fresh-cut
Fresh-from-the-garden
Freshly picked
Frost
Fruit
Fruit tree
Full/partial shade
Full/partial sun

***

Garden
Garden art
Garden space
Gardener
Garden-fresh
Garland
Gather
Germinate
Glorious
Gorgeous
Graceful
Graft

Graft / Grafting
Grass
Graze
Green thumb
Greenhouse
Ground cover
Group
Grove
Grow
Growers
Growth

***

Hand-arranged
Hand-deliver
Hardy
Harvest
Harvest
Healthier
Healthy
Heat
Heavenly
Heavy (with fruit or blossoms)
Herbs
Highlight
Hue
Hybrid

***

Impression
Impressive
In bloom
Indoor
Insect-resistant
Insert
Intensely fragrant
Invasive

***

Jewel-toned
Joyful
Juice

***

Kaleidoscope
Kid-friendly

***

Landscaping
Large
Lasting
Lawn
Leaf
Leaf litter
Lei
Lifeless
Light
Live
Long stem
Long-lasting
Lovely
Low maintenance
Low-growing
Luminous
Lush

***

Magical
Magnificent
Maintain
Maintenance-free
Majestic
Manageable
Mature
Mature
Medicinal
Medley
Mesh strainer (sap)
Mesmerizing
Mingle
Mix
Moisture
Moonlight
Morning

Mosaic
Mow
Mulch
Multicolored
Native
Nestled
Nightfall
Nosegay
Nurture
Nutrients
Nutrients

***

Old
Old-growth
Orchard
Orchard-fresh
Ordinary
Organic
Ornamental
Out of place
Outdoor
Oversized

***

Paired
Paradise
Passionate
Pastel
Pendulous
Perennial
Pests
Petal
Petite
Pick
Plain
Plant
Planter
Plow
Pluck
Plume

Poisonous
Pollen
Pollinate
Popular
Posy
Potpourri
Potting mix
Precious
Preferred
Premium
Pretty
Pristine
Prized
Problem areas
Professional-looking
Propagate
Prune
Pruned
Pure
Purebred

***

Radiant
Rainbow
Rare
Ready-to-bloom
Reap
Recessive
Regal
Reliable
Remove
Replant (with trees)
Rich
Ripen
Rodents
Romantic
Root
Rustic

***

Sag
Sagging
Salt-tolerant
Sap
Scorched
Screen (growth acts like a living screen)
Screening
Seasonal
Seed
Seedling
Select
Selection
Sensible
Sentimental
Serve
Shade
Shade plant
Shade-loving
Shade-tolerant
Shady
Shallow
Ship
Shoot
Show
Showy
Shrub
Silky
Silky-smooth
Single out
Snow
Soft
Soil
Sophisticated
Sort
Sow
Special
Spectacular
Spent

Spray
Spread
Spring
Sprout
Stagger
Statuesque
Steal
Stem
Storage container (for sap)
Striking
Strong-growing
Stunning
Sturdy
Suitable
Summery
Sun
Sun exposure
Sunburst
Sun-kissed
Sun-loving
Sunny
Sunrise
Sunshine
Supplement
Surprise
Sweet
Sweet-smelling
Symbiotic
Symphony

***

Tap
Tapping spiles/spouts (for maple sap)
Tasteless
Tasty
Tend
Tender
Thrive
Thriving
Till

Tolerant
Tolerate
Traditional
Train
Transform
Transplant
Treasure
Treasured
Tree
Tribute
Trim
Trio
Tropical
Tropical-looking
Trunk
Twig

***

Unforgettable
Unique
Unstable
Unusual
Upright
Use
Useful

***

Valley
Variegated
Variety
Vase
Vibrant
Vines
Visual impact
Visually stimulating

***

Water
Watercolor
Weak
Weed
Well-drained

Whimsical
Wilt
Wilted
Window box
Winter
Wither
Withered
Wreath
Wrinkly

***

Yard
Year-round
Yield
Young

***

Zone

53 SCENTS MASTER LIST

Pleasant Scents

Alluring
Amazing
Animal musk
Antiseptic
Appealing
Apple
Aromatic

***

Baby powder
Balanced
Blueberry
Burnt
Burnt/Burned toast

***

Camphor
Cheesy
Chewy
Chocolate
Cinnamon
Citrus (be specific: lemony, lime, orange, grapefruit)
Clean
Clean linen
Cloying

Coconut
Coffee
Cold
Comforting (add the scent of comfort food like mashed
potatoes or curry)
Complex
Cool
Coppery
Cotton candy
Cumin

***

Delicate
Delightful
Different
Distinct
Distinctive
Divine

***

Earthy
Elusive
Enjoyable
Enticing
Excellent
Exotic
Exquisite
Extraordinary

***

Faint
Faintest
Familiar
Fanciful
Fantastic
Fatty
Feminine
Festive
Fishy
Floral
Fragrant
Fresh

Fresh mowed grass
Fruity
Full
Full-bodied

**

Gamy
Garden-fresh
Garlic / Garlicky
Green apple

**

Hand-picked
Harmonious
Healthy
Hearty
Heavenly
Heavy
Herbal

**

Icy
Infused
Intense

**

Jasmine

**

Lasting
Lavender
Leather
Lemon / Lemony
Light
Lilac
Lily
Lily of the valley
Little
Luscious

**

Manly
Marvelous
Masculine
Mashed

Meaty
Medicinal
Mellow
Memorable
Metallic
Mild
Minty
Musk

***

Natural
Nutty

***

Odorless
Old
Onion
Orange
Overpowering
Overwhelming

***

Particular
Pasty
Peach
Peculiar
Pickled
Pine
Plain
Pleasant
Pleasing
Powerful
Pure

***

Refreshing
Regional
Rich
Ripe
Ripened
Roasted
Robust
Rose

Rosemary

***

Sage
Scrumptious
Seductive
Sharp
Smoky
Soothing
Stifling
Strange
Strawberry
Strong
Subtle
Sweet

***

Tantalizing
Tempting
Thick
Tropical

***

Unfamiliar
Unique
Unmistakable

***

Vanilla
Vinegar

***

Warm
Wild
Wonderful
Woodsy
Woody

***

Yeasty

Unpleasant Scents

Acidic
Awful

***

Base

***

Caustic
Curdled

***

Damp
Dank
Decomposing
Dirty (socks)
Disgusting

***

Fecal
Fermented / Fermenting
Festering
Fetid
Foul
Fusty

***

Grody
Gross

***

Infected
Iron

***

Loathsome
Lousy

***

Malodorous
Moldy
Musty

***

Nauseating
Noxious

***

Off
Offensive
Old
Overripe

***

Peculiar
Peppery
Polluted
Pungent
Pustular
Putrescent
Putrid

***

Rancid
Rank
Reek
Repellent
Repugnant
Repulsive
Revolting
Ripe
Rotten
Rotten apples
Rotten eggs
Rotting garbage
Rotting potatoes

***

Sickly
Smelly
Soiled
Sour
Soured
Spoiled
Stagnant
Stale
Stench
Stinking
Stinky
Sulfur

Sweat

***

Tainted
Tinny

***

Unclean
Unpleasant

***

Vile
Vinegary

54 TEXTURE MASTER LIST

Abrasive
Angular
Arid
Attractive

***

Ballooned
Bendable
Bloated
Blunt
Boiling
Broken
Bubbly
Bulky
Bumpy
Burning
Burnished
Bushy

***

Caked
Caressing
Chapped
Cheap
Cheery
Choppy
Clammy

Clean
Coarse
Cold
Complete
Cool
Copious
Corroded
Cottony
Craggy
Crawly
Creamy
Crisp
Crude
Crunchy
Crusty
Cushioned
Cushy

***

Delicate
Disheveled
Downy
Dry
Dull

***

Easy
Elastic
Emblazoned
Engorged
Enlarged
Even
Expanded

***

Feathery
Filmy
Fine
Finished
Firm
Flabby
Flat

Flattened
Fleecy
Fleshy
Flexible
Flimsy
Fluffy
Fluid
Formless
Fragile
Freezing
Frigid
Furry
Fuzzy

***

Gelatinous
Gentle
Glassy
Glazed
Gooey
Goopy
Gossamer
Grainy
Grating
Gravelly
Greasy
Gritty
Gunky

***

Hairy
Hard
Harsh
Hatched
Healthy
Heavy
Hoarse

***

Icy
Ill-Defined
Imperfect

Imprinted
Incline
Incomplete
Indented
Inflexible
Inset
Inviting
Irregular
Itchy

***

Jagged
Jumbled

***

Knobby
Knotty

***

Layered
Limp
Long
Lukewarm

***

Malleable
Matte
Mellifluous
Mild
Milky
Mucky
Mutilated

***

Numbing

***

Oily

***

Piercing
Pliable
Plump
Pointed
Polished
Potholed

Powdery
Prickly
Pulpy

***

Raised
Raw
Refined
Restful
Ridged
Rigid
Rocky
Rough
Ruffled
Rugged
Rusty

***

Scaled
Scorching
Scored
Scraggy
Scratched
Scratchy
Sculptured
Serrated
Set In
Severe
Shaggy
Sharp
Sheen
Short
Silken
Silky
Sleek
Slick
Slimy
Slippery
Slovenly
Smooth
Smoothed

Smudged
Snug
Sodden
Soft
Solid
Sparkling
Spiky / Spikes
Spiny
Spongy
Spotless
Sprawling
Springy
Steely
Steep
Stiff
Still
Stony
Strong
Substantial
Supple
Sweltering
Swollen
Syrupy

***

Tangled
Thick
Thin
Tidy
Tiled
Tough
Translucent

***

Uncomfortable
Uncompromising
Unequal
Uneven
Unfinished
Unsoiled
Untainted

***

Vague
Varnished
Velvety
Veneered
Viscous
Vivacious

***

Warm
Wavy
Welcoming
Well-Defined
Well-Honed
Wet
Whetted
Wholesome
Wide
Withered
Wooden
Woolen
Woolly
Worn
Woven
Wrinkled

***

Yielding

55 WATER MASTER LIST

Absorbent

***

Blue
Boiling
Brackish
Briny
Brown
Bubbly

***

Calm
Chaotic
Choppy
Cleansing
Clear
Clear
Coastal
Cold
Conductive
Contaminated
Crystal
Crystalline
Current

***

Dangerous
Deadly

Deep-Sea

***

Edible
Emotional
Ever-Moving

***

Fetid
Flat
Fluid
Foam (Ocean)
Forbidding
Foul
Fresh
Freshwater
Frozen

***

Glassy
Gleaming
Glistening
Glittering
Green

***

Hard
Hazardous
Healthy
Heavy
High
High tide

***

Icy
Illusive
Influencing
Inshore

***

Limited
Liquid
Low
Low-Tides
Lucent

Luminous

***

Marine
Material
Medium
Mirrored
Muddy
Murky
Mystical

***

Navigable
Non-Living

***

Oceanic
Odorless
Offshore

***

Pacific
Passable
Pelagic
Poisonous
Powerful
Precious
Prismatic

***

Radiant
Rampant
Reflective
Refreshing
Responsive
Rough

***

Salty
Shapeless
Shimmering
Shiny
Slime Infested
Sloppy
Slow Running

Smooth
Smothering
Soft
Sparkling
Squishy
Stagnant
Stinking
Swollen

***

Thirst quenching
Threatening
Tranquil

***

Untamed

***

Vapid
Viscous

***

Warm
Wavy
Welcoming
Wet
Wild
Winding
Wondrous

ABOUT THE AUTHOR

Piper writes genre fiction under another pen name. The contents of this book has been very helpful for her career and she wanted to share her knowledge with other authors.

If you would like to receive an email when the next book will be available, you can email her at piperbradley35@gmail.com

Piper is not using a mailing list because lately they have been notoriously unreliable.